Family Tree Workbook

BRIAN SHEFFEY

Family Tree Workbook

30+ Step-by-Step Worksheets
to Build Your Family History

**ROCKRIDGE
PRESS**

For general information on our other products and services or to obtain technical support, please contact our Customer Care Department within the United States at (866) 744-2665, or outside the United States at (510) 253-0500.

Rockridge Press publishes its books in a variety of electronic and print formats. Some content that appears in print may not be available in electronic books, and vice versa.

Interior and Cover Designer: John Calmeyer
Art Producer: Tom Hood
Editor: Andrea Leptinsky
Production Editor: Nora Milman

Author photo courtesy of Alexis Yeldell-Williams

ISBN: Print 978-1-64611-608-9

R0

To the family and colleagues
who have supported me
in my genealogy adventures
who are no longer with us.
In loving memory.

CONTENTS

INTRODUCTION

Family history research is an exciting endeavor that dives deep into the details of relatives' lives dating back decades, if not hundreds of years. What does that mean for a family history researcher? It's paramount to organize all the discovered information as concisely as possible.

As a family history researcher begins uncovering information, one can easily overlook the importance of organization. The allure of discovering new relatives and connecting their life history "dots" can be hard to dismiss, when it comes time to pause and record (and preserve) all the gathered information. After all, that *is* how you create your family tree!

The best time to start making a habit of organizing and recording family history is now, at the beginning of your research. The *Family Tree Workbook* helps you do one basic thing: capture important genealogical information in a format that is easy for you to refer to in the course of your research. Essentially, it serves as a research log that includes:

- A comprehensive list of sources you have used to research an ancestor;
- A tool to identify areas for future research (identified through missing pieces of information, like an ancestor's place of birth);
- A summary of your research discoveries;
- An overview of where you have stored or saved copies of documents you have accessed and used;
- A place for your notes about the sources of information you have used in your search, whether you found the information you needed or not;
- A place to put your notations about your research strategies and suggestions about future areas of research you peruse; your questions; your analysis about your research and research strategies; and any information discrepancies you uncover along the way.

The *Family Tree Workbook* is flexible enough to use for documenting either one ancestor's life, or that of an entire family group. What's better is that you can easily pass this down to future generations to continue research and create an invaluable family heirloom.

Packed with handy worksheets, this workbook will give you the different types of worksheets you need to capture information about your ancestors—and keep that information safe.

Best of luck on your new journey toward uncovering and documenting your family history!

HOW TO USE THIS BOOK

This family tree workbook supports you in organizing your family's genealogy. Simple instructions, a pedigree chart, family group worksheets, and other sheets will help you log information from a variety of records and documents.

> Use these forms regularly. Make copies of the worksheets before you begin inputting your information.

Each worksheet has a reference number to make it easier to refer to them in the other sheets. For instance, use the Ancestor Overview (page 4) worksheet as a master worksheet where you jot down all the other forms on which you've added the same ancestor's information. This eliminates flicking through a whole book or multiple worksheets to find other places you've added your second great grandparents.

This workbook is arranged so you do not have to work your way through it sequentially. However, familiarize yourself with the foundation concepts and worksheets in Part 1 to assist you with the first part of your genealogy research.

Workbook Guidance

The workbook is arranged in five parts:

PART 1 provides you with a blank pedigree chart to fill in, along with forms to complete for members of your immediate family. There are also migration maps for you to chart your family's movement across the United States.

PART 2 covers logging information from a variety of forms—from marriage records to deeds of sale for enslaved people to information about Native American ancestors. There are also worksheets to use when you begin interviewing family members. There are also forms for you to use to work with your DNA results.

PART 3 covers U.S. Census records as well as a form that documents the arrival of immigrant ancestors.

PART 4 acts as an information quality checklist. The sheets will help you spot discrepancies in an ancestor's name, or their date and place of birth. You will also easily see any gaps in information you have for an ancestor, like their date and place of death, or when they married their second spouse.

PART 5 covers troubleshooting common research problems, as well as a form for keeping your research safe.

While this book is designed for you to use alongside Rockridge Press's *Practical Genealogy: 50 Simple Steps to Research Your Diverse Family History*, it's also the perfect stand-alone workbook for any genealogist to capture important ancestral information.

Familiarize yourself with all the worksheets in this book. Pay attention to what information each worksheet is asking you to include and how each worksheet may relate to others in this book. Decide whether you will use this book to document the life of a single ancestor or a single family, as this workbook allows for both approaches. Decide what you wish to accomplish.

Now it's time to dive into the worksheets!

A Quick Note on Adoptive, IVF, Step-, Same-Sex, and Non-Binary Parented Family Research

Worksheets in this book are adaptable to fit individual research needs. Start with the Blended Family Worksheet (page 15) if your research involves an adoptive, IVF, same-sex, or non-binary parented family. Use the Blended Family Worksheet to capture information for people in households with one biological parent and one non-biological parent. Additionally, you can use the same form for adoptees who want to note information about their adopted family as well as their biological family.

The remaining forms, notably the fan chart, are there for you to add information about the biological family you are researching. You may wish to maintain two separate workbooks—one for your non-biological family research and a second for your biological family research.

PART 1

Individual and Family-Specific Worksheets

Standard family tree research forms, like the following individual and family-specific worksheets, are the primary way to record and keep track of information for your family tree. In Part 1, you'll not only log information on the specific members of your family, but also where they've lived on a map. Seeing your family history in action is about to begin!

Pedigree Chart

A pedigree chart is made up of blank cells where you add the names of your direct maternal and paternal ancestors. Each cell contains a number that acts like a unique fingerprint. Each direct ancestor will have a unique reference number that you will use on all the family tree worksheets. This reference number is included with an ancestor's name as you place their information on the various worksheets.

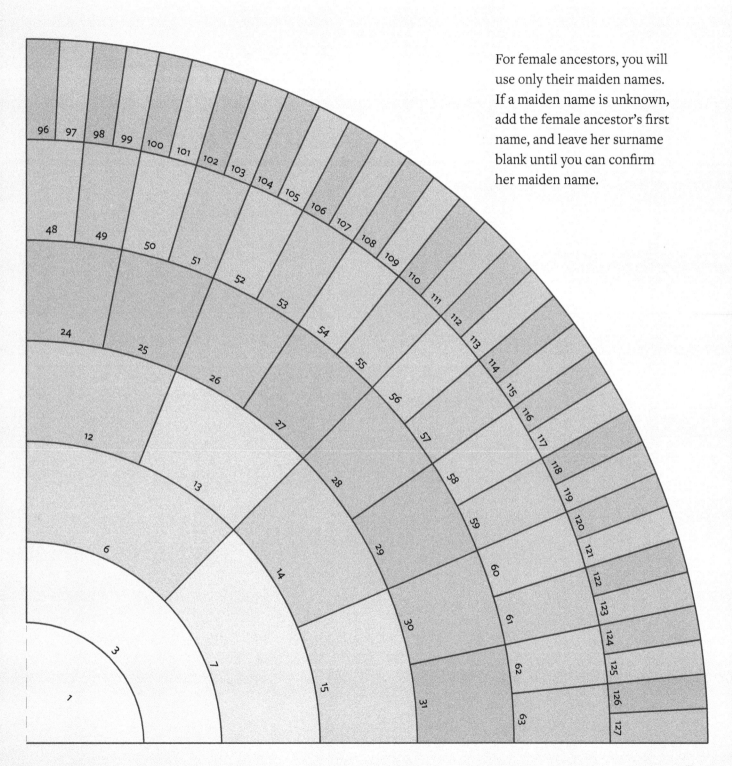

For female ancestors, you will use only their maiden names. If a maiden name is unknown, add the female ancestor's first name, and leave her surname blank until you can confirm her maiden name.

Ancestor Overview Worksheet

The Ancestor Overview Worksheet builds on the information you have written in the Ancestor Fan Chart. This worksheet offers you an overview of your parents' family group over a three-generation period. You can find more generations for download at www.callistomedia books.com/familytreeworkbook.

Fill in the information about your parents, grandparents, and other relatives, and make sure that you include their family reference number from your pedigree chart. This helps you stay organized. You will add Fan Chart Family Reference numbers to other worksheets. This will help you keep track of hundreds of individuals in the various worksheets you will create.

On the top right of the worksheet you will see a space that is marked "Family Surname." This will help you quickly organize your worksheets

by a family's surname, if that is your working preference.

The Ancestor Overview Worksheet is in two parts. Worksheet 2A covers the first three sets of generational grandparents in your father's lineage. Worksheet 2B covers the first three sets of generational grandparents in your mother's lineage.

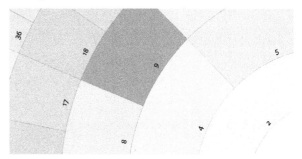

Figure 1: *In the example above, the individual in Cell #9 will always be the same person. This will always be this individual's Family Reference # (e.g., Paul Smith, Family Ref. #9)*

Paternal Pedigree

Family Surname:_____

Father's Pedigree *(Fan Chart Ref. #:_____)*	
Generation 1	Birth Name:
	Known As / Nickname:
	Date of Birth:
	Birth Place:
	Date of Death:
	Death Place:
	Occupation:
	Added to Worksheets:

Paternal Grandfather
(Fan Chart Ref. #: _____)

Generation 2

Birth Name:

Known As / Nickname:

Date of Birth:

Birth Place:

Date of Death:

Death Place:

Occupation:

Added to Worksheets:

Paternal Grandmother
(Fan Chart Ref. #: _____)

Birth Name:

Known As / Nickname:

Date of Birth:

Birth Place:

Date of Death:

Death Place:

Occupation:

Added to Worksheets:

Paternal Great Grandfather
(Fan Chart Ref. #: _____)

Generation 3

Birth Name:

Known As / Nickname:

Date of Birth:

Birth Place:

Date of Death:

Death Place:

Occupation:

Added to Worksheets:

Paternal Great Grandmother
(Fan Chart Ref. #: _____)

Birth Name:

Known As / Nickname:

Date of Birth:

Birth Place:

Date of Death:

Death Place:

Occupation:

Added to Worksheets:

Maternal Pedigree

Family Surname:_____

Mother's Pedigree *(Fan Chart Ref. #: _____)*

Generation 1	
	Birth Name:
	Known As / Nickname:
	Date of Birth:
	Birth Place:
	Date of Death:
	Death Place:
	Occupation:
	Added to Worksheets:

Maternal Grandfather
(Fan Chart Ref. #: _____)

Generation 2

Birth Name:

Known As / Nickname:

Date of Birth:

Birth Place:

Date of Death:

Death Place:

Occupation:

Added to Worksheets:

Maternal Grandmother
(Fan Chart Ref. #: _____)

Birth Name:

Known As / Nickname:

Date of Birth:

Birth Place:

Date of Death:

Death Place:

Occupation:

Added to Worksheets:

Maternal Great Grandfather
(Fan Chart Ref. #: _____)

Generation 3

Birth Name:

Known As / Nickname:

Date of Birth:

Birth Place:

Date of Death:

Death Place:

Occupation:

Added to Worksheets:

Maternal Great Grandmother
(Fan Chart Ref. #: _____)

Birth Name:

Known As / Nickname:

Date of Birth:

Birth Place:

Date of Death:

Death Place:

Occupation:

Added to Worksheets:

Family Address Worksheet

Building on the information you gathered for the Ancestor Overview Worksheet (page 4), an address worksheet is a useful way to keep track of the last place of residence for an ancestor. The Family Address Worksheet allows you to easily capture and retain information about where four generations of your ancestors last lived.

You should also take an ancestor's previous addresses into consideration. To include an ancestor's previous residential addresses, you can:

→ Write the older address(es) on the back of the worksheet; or

→ Write the address(es) on a separate sheet of paper, and attach those extra sheets to this worksheet; or

→ Find city directories that reference your ancestors, which will contain their home addresses. Print them and attach to this worksheet. _____

Family Address Worksheets are a convenient way to keep track of where your ancestors were living so you can easily access this information when you need it. Knowing where an ancestor lived and died will enable you to locate records and documents better. Using information sources like local newspapers, local newsletters, local organizational records, or local government records, you will be armed with the names of the towns, counties, and states where they lived, thus narrowing the scope of where you will need to search for documents.

Next, you can move on to the Family Group Worksheet, where you will be adding more family information.

Ancestor Address Worksheet

Family Surname: _____

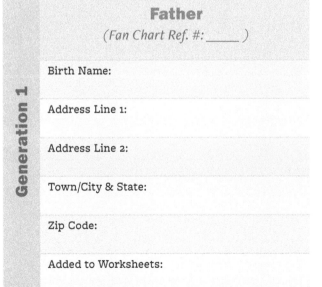

	Father (Fan Chart Ref. #: _____)	**Mother** (Fan Chart Ref. #: _____)
Generation 1	Birth Name:	Birth Name:
	Address Line 1:	Address Line 1:
	Address Line 2:	Address Line 2:
	Town/City & State:	Town/City & State:
	Zip Code:	Zip Code:
	Added to Worksheets:	Added to Worksheets:

Paternal Grandfather
(Fan Chart Ref. #: _____)

Birth Name:

Address Line 1:

Address Line 2:

Town/City & State:

Zip Code:

Added to Worksheets:

Maternal Grandfather
(Fan Chart Ref. #: _____)

Birth Name:

Address Line 1:

Address Line 2:

Town/City & State:

Zip Code:

Added to Worksheets:

Paternal Grandmother
(Fan Chart Ref. #: _____)

Birth Name:

Address Line 1:

Address Line 2:

Town/City & State:

Zip Code:

Added to Worksheets:

Maternal Grandmother
(Fan Chart Ref. #: _____)

Birth Name:

Address Line 1:

Address Line 2:

Town/City & State:

Zip Code:

Added to Worksheets:

CONTINUED ON NEXT PAGE

Generation 3

Paternal Great Grandfather
(Fan Chart Ref. #: _____)

Birth Name:

Address Line 1:

Address Line 2:

Town/City & State:

Zip Code:

Added to Worksheets:

Maternal Great Grandfather
(Fan Chart Ref. #: _____)

Birth Name:

Address Line 1:

Address Line 2:

Town/City & State:

Zip Code:

Added to Worksheets:

Paternal Great Grandmother
(Fan Chart Ref. #: _____)

Birth Name:

Address Line 1:

Address Line 2:

Town/City & State:

Zip Code:

Added to Worksheets:

Maternal Great Grandmother
(Fan Chart Ref. #: _____)

Birth Name:

Address Line 1:

Address Line 2:

Town/City & State:

Zip Code:

Added to Worksheets:

Family Group Worksheet

Family Surname:_____

The Family Group Worksheet lets you add information about a nuclear family group consisting of parents and their children. There is space to include two parents and children. You can add an ancestor's additional marriage(s) and children to the Blended Family Worksheet (page 15) in this workbook to capture information about other spouses, stepchildren, and step-siblings.

In this worksheet, you will add additional family members, namely an ancestor's siblings, for the first time. You will now start to expand your family tree beyond your direct line ancestors. This worksheet gives you a convenient overview of a single-family group that you can use to document details for each of your ancestral family groups. It is a worksheet that you will want to copy and print, to have spare copies.

If you need to add more children, you can add them to the back of the worksheet. Or you can use the Sibling Worksheet (page 13) to add an ancestor's additional children if they had more children.

Remember, a seven-generation pedigree chart has 14 couples, which means that you will have 14 separate family group sheets, one for each couple. Make copies of the blank forms in *The Family Tree Workbook* before you fill them in.

CONTINUED ON NEXT PAGE

	Father	**Mother**
	(Fan Chart Ref. #:_____)	*(Fan Chart Ref. #:_____)*
Parents	Birth Name:	Birth Name:
	Known As / Nickname:	Known As / Nickname:
	Date of Birth:	Date of Birth:
	Birth Place:	Birth Place:
	Occupation:	Occupation:
	Marriage Date:	Marriage Date:
	Marriage Place:	Marriage Place:
	Added to Worksheets:	Added to Worksheets:

(Family Group Ref. #: _____)

Child 1

Birth Name:

Known As / Nickname:

Date of Birth:

Birth Place:

Male/Female:

Occupation:

Spouse:

Death Date:

Place of Death:

Added to Worksheets:

(Family Group Ref. #: _____)

Child 2

Birth Name:

Known As / Nickname:

Date of Birth:

Birth Place:

Male/Female:

Occupation:

Spouse:

Death Date:

Place of Death:

Added to Worksheets:

(Family Group Ref. #: _____)

Child 3

Birth Name:

Known As / Nickname:

Date of Birth:

Birth Place:

Male/Female:

Occupation:

Spouse:

Death Date:

Place of Death:

Added to Worksheets:

(Family Group Ref. #: _____)

Child 4

Birth Name:

Known As / Nickname:

Date of Birth:

Birth Place:

Male/Female:

Occupation:

Spouse:

Death Date:

Place of Death:

Added to Worksheets:

Sibling Worksheet

Family Surname:_____

The Sibling Worksheet documents the siblings for each of your matrilineal and patrilineal ancestors. The big difference between this worksheet and the Family Group Worksheet (page 11) is that you will now be entering information about an ancestor's sibling's children (that is, your ancestor's nieces and nephews). Once again, you will want to make a copy of the blank worksheet before you start to enter information.

This is a worksheet that you will need to complete for all of an ancestor's siblings. For instance, if Jack Jones had seven brothers and sisters, you will need a separate copy of this worksheet for each of his seven siblings. There is space for you to add references to other worksheets, such as an ancestor's siblings. This will enable you to track specific individuals from worksheet to worksheet.

Once you complete this worksheet, you can review the Blended Family Worksheet (page 15), where you can enter information about stepsiblings, adopted siblings, and foster siblings.

Tip

You can also use this worksheet as a "spillover" for the Family Group Worksheet if there are more children within a family group.

CONTINUED ON NEXT PAGE

Father
(Fan Chart Ref. #: _____)

Parents	
	Birth Name:
	Known As / Nickname:
	Date of Birth:
	Birth Place:
	Occupation:
	Marriage Date:
	Marriage Place:
	Added to Worksheets:

Mother
(Fan Chart Ref. #: _____)

Birth Name:
Known As / Nickname:
Date of Birth:
Birth Place:
Occupation:
Marriage Date:
Marriage Place:
Added to Worksheets:

(Family Group Ref. #: _____)

Child 1

Birth Name:

Known As / Nickname:

Date of Birth:

Birth Place:

Male/Female:

Occupation:

Spouse:

Death Date:

Place of Death:

Added to Worksheets:

(Family Group Ref. #: _____)

Child 2

Birth Name:

Known As / Nickname:

Date of Birth:

Birth Place:

Male/Female:

Occupation:

Spouse:

Death Date:

Place of Death:

Added to Worksheets:

(Family Group Ref. #: _____)

Child 3

Birth Name:

Known As / Nickname:

Date of Birth:

Birth Place:

Male/Female:

Occupation:

Spouse:

Death Date:

Place of Death:

Added to Worksheets:

(Family Group Ref. #: _____)

Child 4

Birth Name:

Known As / Nickname:

Date of Birth:

Birth Place:

Male/Female:

Occupation:

Spouse:

Death Date:

Place of Death:

Added to Worksheets:

Blended Family Worksheet

Family Surname:_____

This worksheet has been created for you to capture information about individuals who were or are members of blended families. **This includes adoptive, IVF, step-, same-sex couples, and non-binary parented families.** You will be able to add an ancestor's new spouse, as well as children a second or third spouse may have had with their previous spouse(s). The form is also flexible enough to document households that have a biological and a non-biological parent.

There is also space to add information about stepchildren, as well as adopted or foster children.

Time to Reflect

Check in with your research process by answering the following questions:

∗ How well do you understand the concept of pedigree charts and how they differ from family trees?

∗ How confident are you in keeping your research and research materials organized?

∗ Do you understand why maiden names are important?

Give yourself permission to acknowledge if you are still unclear about a topic that we have explored together. Reread a previous step, or parts of step sections, if necessary. Remember, genealogy is an endurance activity. It isn't a sprint.

(Ancestor's Ref. #:_____)

Ancestor

Birth Name:

Known As / Nickname:

Date of Birth:

Birth Place:

Occupation:

Marriage Date:

Marriage Place:

Added to Worksheets:

(Ancestor's Ref. #:_____)

New Spouse (Step-Parent)

Birth Name:

Known As / Nickname:

Date of Birth:

Birth Place:

Occupation:

Marriage Date:

Marriage Place:

Added to Worksheets:

CONTINUED ON NEXT PAGE

(Family Group
Ref. #: _____)

(Family Group
Ref. #: _____)

(Family Group
Ref. #: _____)

Half Sibling

Birth Name:

Known As / Nickname:

Date of Birth:

Birth Place:

Male/Female:

Occupation:

Spouse:

Marriage Date:

Marriage Place:

Death Date:

Place of Death:

Added to Worksheets:

Half Sibling

Birth Name:

Known As / Nickname:

Date of Birth:

Birth Place:

Male/Female:

Occupation:

Spouse:

Marriage Date:

Marriage Place:

Death Date:

Place of Death:

Added to Worksheets:

Adopted or Foster Child

Birth Name:

Known As / Nickname:

Date of Birth:

Birth Place:

Male/Female:

Occupation:

Spouse:

Marriage Date:

Marriage Place:

Death Date:

Place of Death:

Added to Worksheets:

Step-Child

Birth Name:

Known As / Nickname:

Date of Birth:

Birth Place:

Male/Female:

Occupation:

Spouse:

Marriage Date:

Marriage Place:

Death Date:

Place of Death:

Added to Worksheets:

Step-Child

Birth Name:

Known As / Nickname:

Date of Birth:

Birth Place:

Male/Female:

Occupation:

Spouse:

Marriage Date:

Marriage Place:

Death Date:

Place of Death:

Added to Worksheets:

Step-Child

Birth Name:

Known As / Nickname:

Date of Birth:

Birth Place:

Male/Female:

Occupation:

Spouse:

Marriage Date:

Marriage Place:

Death Date:

Place of Death:

Added to Worksheets:

Family Group Timeline

Use the Family Group Timeline worksheet to create a quick timeline for a family group. Use this worksheet to visualize and depict specific information you have collected in the preceding worksheets.

If you begin to struggle to piece together an ancestor's life, creating a timeline can help you visualize the problem. Whatever the missing piece of information is, understanding the information gap will help you determine what records, documents, or other resources you need to track down in order to provide the data you need to plug a gap.

One of the reasons you may have an information gap in your family tree, or lose track of a family altogether, is because they moved from one county to another, or they may have moved to a different state. Tracking family migration journeys will be the next topic that you explore.

Family Member Names (include their Ref. # plus dates of birth and death)	Year (e.g., 1830)	Year (e.g., 1840)
Joe Bloggs (22) b. 1835 : d. 1880	b. 1835, Halifax County, VA	1849 — Saves brother Jim from drowning

Key Life Moments & Events

Year (e.g., 1850)	Year (e.g., 1860)	Year (e.g., 1870)	Year (e.g., 1880)	Year (e.g., 1890)
1850 — attended Richmond Farming School	1868 — buys 200-acre farm, Woodford County, KY	1871 — marriage to Jane Smythe (KY)	1880 — death in Woodford County, KY	

U.S. Family Migration Map

Family Surname:_____

Family migration maps help you visualize a journey that your ancestors made across the U.S. while signaling to you new records to search for as you plot their route. They are fun to work with, as every journey is an adventure. Working with maps like this really brings that adventure home.

There is a practical benefit to working with a migration map. Researching the major migration routes that crisscrossed the growing U.S. can tell you about the major stopping points. You can discover places where a pioneering family would have rested before undergoing the next stage of their migration. Each resting place could be a location that has records about the family you are researching.

Additionally, use the following World Family Migration Map (page 22) to trace the journey that ancestors undertook when they left their native land behind for a new life in the American colonies and the United States.

Family Group Members' Names (include the individual ancestor reference numbers)	Migration Year	Migration Path Color

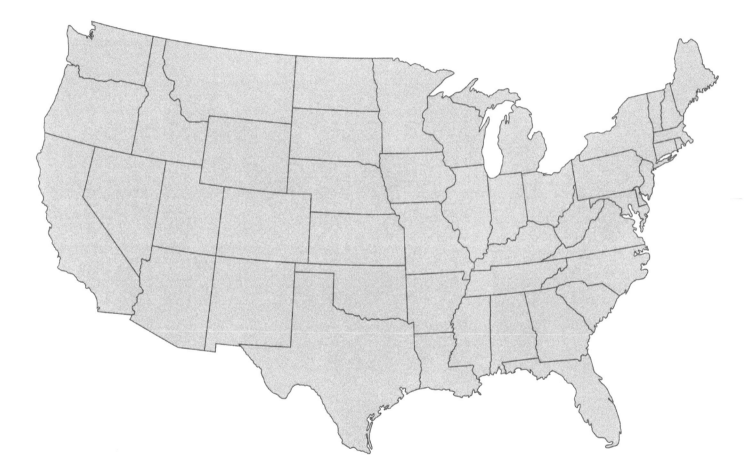

Key

○	Departure Location	– – – – – –	Journey by Train
△	Arrival Location	— · — · — ·	Journey by Plane
☆	Burial Location	·· — ·· — ·· — ··	Journey by Wagon
————	Journey by Car	· · · · · · · ·	Journey by Horse
— — — —	Journey by Boat	··············	Journey by Foot

World Family Migration Map

Family Surname:_____

Like the U.S. Family Migration Map Work-sheet (page 20), the World Family Migration Map Worksheet helps you visualize the journey that a family made from the "Old Country" to the United States. Like the previous Family Migration Map, you can differentiate the various migration stages by using contrasting colors to reflect the stages of an overall journey.

Key				
○	Departure Location	– – – – –	Journey by Train
△	Arrival Location	– · – · –	Journey by Plane
☆	Burial Location	·· – ·· – ··	Journey by Wagon
─────	Journey by Car	· · · · · ·	Journey by Horse
– – – –	Journey by Boat	··············	Journey by Foot

Family Group Members' Names (include the individual ancestor reference numbers)	Migration Year	Migration Path Color

Time to Reflect

Check in with yourself by answering the following questions:

* How successful have you been in finding your ancestor's basic information?

* Using your completed forms, how confident are you in identifying possible places to locate necessary records that provide information about your ancestors (e.g., county- or state-level records, archives)?

* How confident are you when it comes to identifying gaps in information and working out strategies to locate and access that information?

* How confident are you in keeping your research and research materials organized?

* How confident are you that you can use maps to answer some of your research questions?

Allow yourself to really understand and apply the fundamental introductory concepts you have explored up to this point.

PART 2

Compiling Information

While it's vital that you keep all your family tree research organized, it's also equally as important that you log, and ultimately preserve, the information you discover in the most appropriate manner. From marriage and military records to storing family photos, the following worksheets will help you save the valuable information you've uncovered for years to come.

Marriage Records

Family Surname:

_____

Your family tree may be filled with hidden stories of marriages forged through political unions, the merger of two local dynasties, scandalous elopements, or romantic courtships. Marriage records are one clue you will need to unlock those hidden histories and bring them to light.

When completing the marriage record worksheet, don't forget to include the resources you used to find your ancestor's marriage record (e.g., FamilySearch, local archive, state archive), and details about where you found a marriage document (e.g., Henrico County Marriages, Book A, 1759–1808, p. 113). Entering many details—especially where you found a marriage record—will help you to keep your research organized. It will also save you time not to retrace your research steps by eliminating another search to find the same record.

Groom or Person 1 (include age at the time of marriage)	Bride or Person 2 (include age at the time of marriage)	Marriage Bond (include place and date of bond)	Bondsmen Cited in Marriage Bond (a term used in older marriage records)

Marriage Date	Marriage Town, County, and State	Marriage Witnesses	Source Used and Its Location	Source Details (e.g., microfilm #, file folder #, and location of source)

Land Deed Index

Family Surname:

_____

You can learn more about your family from land deeds, which can tell you some unexpected details about your family and fill in some gaps in your family tree. The Land Deed Index Worksheet makes it easy to track land ownership within a family group. Once you have completed the Land Index Worksheet, there's another set of land records to consider: War Service Bounty Land Warrants. To learn if your ancestors qualified for such a land warrant, you will need to find and log information about their military service, which is the next subject to explore.

Landowner's Name (with Family Ref. #)	Deed #	Date of Deed
Ezekiel Harlan	A-6	19 Feb 1722

Land Description	Location of Land	Grantor (Seller)
Adjoining Marr's land, Br. of Marsh Run	King George County (plotted N-S-E-W map location reference not supplied)	William Allen

CONTINUED ON NEXT PAGE

Grantee (Buyer)	Record Source	Record Location	File Page #
Christopher Marr	Virginia Northern Neck Land Grants, 1694–1742. Vol. I Book A	Library of Virginia, Richmond, Virginia	Page 13

CONTINUED FROM PREVIOUS PAGE

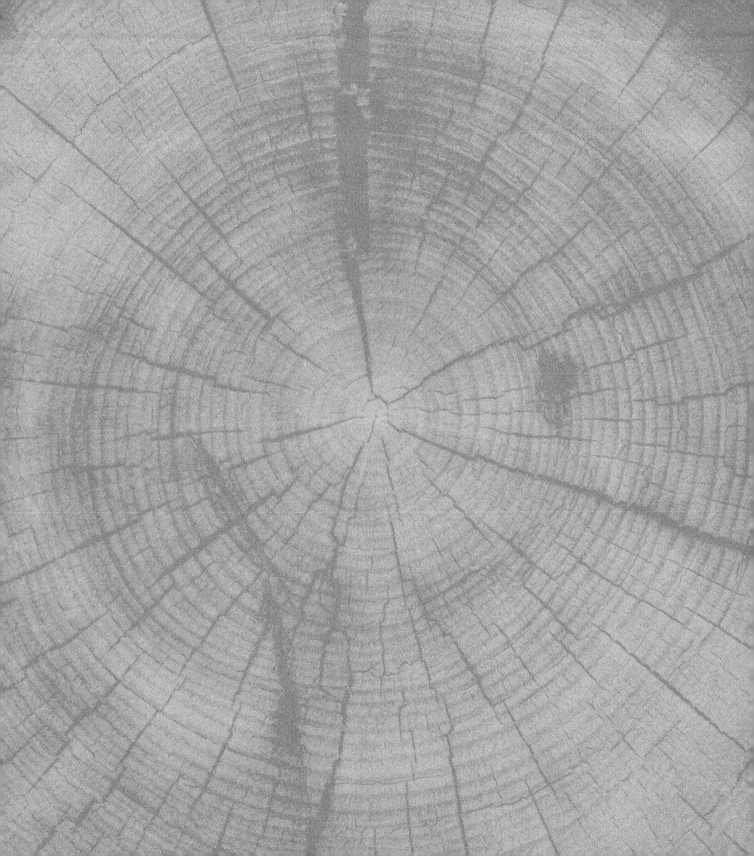

Military History Checklist

Family Surname:

_____

The Military Service Checklist in this worksheet allows you to efficiently track military service within your family. This checklist acts as an overview to assist you in logging ancestors who served in the military. An additional Military Service Log worksheet allows you to note more details about the wars and conflicts where an ancestor fought.

Indicate with an ✕ or ✓ in the boxes for family members who fought in the conflicts listed.

▨ _Check state records_
◉ _Check federal records_

Ancestor Name and Family Ref. # (plus birth and death dates and military rank)	Colonial Wars ▨	American Revolution 1775–1783 ▨ ◉	1784–1811	War of 1812 1812–1815	Native American Wars 1815–1858

Patriot War 1838	Mexican War 1846–1848	Civil War 1861–1865	Buffalo Soldier Military Service 1866–1951	Spanish-American War 1898–1899	Philippine Insurrection 1899–1902	World War I 1917–1918	World War II 1941–1945	Vietnam War 1955–1975	Granada Invasion 25 Oct 1983 – 15 Dec 1983	Panama Invasion 1989–1990	Gulf War 1990–1991	Afghanistan War 2001–	Iraq War 2003–

Military Service Log

Family Surname:

_____

The Military Service Log is a follow-up worksheet to the Military History Checklist (page 32). You will see that there is more space for you to add further information for an ancestor's military service, including a space for any wartime stories you discovered in your research. This is information you will definitely want to add to your family tree. Researching an ancestor's military service is a great way to honor an ancestor's memory, as well as their service to their country.

Write the service information, as well as relevant genealogical information, in the provided spaces. You can add more service information to the back of the worksheet. You may also fasten copies of photographs and military service documents to this worksheet.

Ancestor Name and Ref. # (plus birth and death dates)	Military Service Branch	Service Dates

Rank & Service Unit	Conflicts Served in	Battles	Awards & Military Decorations	War Stories (You can add stories to supplemental sheets that you can attach to this worksheet)	Information Sources

Family Medical History

Family Surname:

_____

Knowing your family's medical history will give you insights into common family health conditions. Your family's medical history is hidden in your family tree until you bring it to light through medical-related records and documents like mortality schedules and death certificates. You can use this family medical history to understand risk factors for certain health conditions.

The Family Medical History Worksheet enables you to record three generations of illnesses and medical conditions within your family.

Indicate with an ✗ or ✓ in the boxes for family members who have had any of the following medical conditions:

Tip

Interview your immediate family members about health conditions experienced by your parents, grandparents, and great grandparents, as well as their respective siblings. You can also consult the following documents for health-related information about your ancestors:

* family medical records;
* old family letters;
* obituaries or funeral programs;
* mortality schedules; and
* death certificates.

Medical Condition	Alcoholism	Allergies (General)	Allergies (Food)	Alzheimer's / Dementia / Memory Issues
Mom				
Dad				
Your Sister				
Your Brother				
Son				
Daughter				
Maternal Grandmother				
Maternal Grandfather				
Mom's Brother				
Mom's Sister				
Paternal Grandfather				
Paternal Grandmother				
Father's Brother				
Father's Sister				

Anesthesia Problems	Anxiety / Panic Attacks / PTSD	Arthritis	Asthma	Blood Issues / Clotting Disorder	Bone / Joint Problems	Cancer (Breast / Ovarian)	Cancer (Prostate / Testicular)	Cancer (Other)	Colitis / IBS / Colon Issues	Depression	Diabetes	Ear / Nose / Throat Problem	Eczema / Psoriasis	Epilepsy / Seizures	Fertility Issues

CONTINUED ON NEXT PAGE

CONTINUED FROM PREVIOUS PAGE

Medical Condition	Gallbladder / Gallstones	Glaucoma / Cataracts / Eye Issues	Gynecological Issues	Hay Fever	Headaches / Migraines	Hearing Problems / Hearing Loss	Heart Problems (Angina, Murmur, etc.)	Hepatitis A, B, or C	High Blood Pressure	High Cholesterol	Hypoglycemia	Kidney Disease	Leukemia	Liver Disease
Mom														
Dad														
Your Sister														
Your Brother														
Son														
Daughter														
Maternal Grandmother														
Maternal Grandfather														
Mom's Brother														
Mom's Sister														
Paternal Grandfather														
Paternal Grandmother														
Father's Brother														
Father's Sister														

Low Blood Pressure	Lung Disease	Rheumatism	Shingles	Sickle Cell Anemia	Stroke	Tay Sachs	Thyroid Disease	Tonsillitis	Tuberculosis	Tumors or Growths	Ulcers	Vitamin Deficiency (e.g., Pellagra)	Other _____	Other _____	Other _____

Death Record Search Log

Family Surname:

_____

Death records can tell you more about your ancestor than simply where they died. Death certificates, mortality schedules, obituaries, funeral home records, and funeral programs can include a wealth of information about a deceased person, including:

- the names of their parents;
- the names of their surviving spouse and children;
- the names of their siblings;
- the name of the informant, or the name of the person who provided details about your ancestor for a death record (this person may or may not be your ancestor's relative, which you will need to research);
- where an ancestor and their family members were living at the time the ancestor died;
- when and where your ancestor was born—and where they died;
- your ancestor's occupation;
- possible military service; and
- cause of death.

Name of Deceased:

Gender:

Family Ref. #:

Date of Death (MMDDYYYY):

Marital Status at Time of Death:

Occupation:

Cause of Death:

Informant:

Informant's Relationship to the Deceased:

Mortuary:

Cemetery:

Military Burial:

County Death Record Book Details

Death Certificate #:	Book Vol:	Book Page:

Residence at Date of Death

Address:

County:	Town/City:	State:

Place of Death
(if different from residence location)

Location:

County:	Town/City:	State:

Parents' Details

Father's Name:	Mother's Name:

Father's Birth Place:	Mother's Birth Place:

Cemetery Research Log

Family Surname:

_____

Date Visited:

_____

You can uncover quite a bit of important information from a headstone. The Cemetery Research Log documents the important genealogical information you will discover at the cemetery where your family is buried.

How to Best Use This Worksheet

Take the log with you when you visit the cemetery. After you find the headstones you're seeking, take a few moments to fill out this worksheet.

Record the cemetery's name and location. The worksheet has space to include the section and lot number for the burials you are documenting. These will help you find the graves and accompanying headstones again.

Record all information from the headstone. This includes birth and death dates. Also, write down any inscriptions from the headstones.

Take a picture of the stone. You can print your pictures and attach the printouts to the Cemetery Research Log Worksheet. This will enable you to remember which tombstone(s) to look for if you need to find them again.

Look for nearby stones that feature the same surname(s) as the one you're researching. They may be related! You can write this information on the back of the Cemetery Research Log.

Name of Cemetery:

Cemetery Phone #:

Street Address:

City/Town:

County:

State:

Name of Ancestor (with Family Ref. #)	Date of Birth	Date of Death	Age at Time of Death	Tombstone Inscription	Location in Cemetery				Photograph Taken? (Y or N)
					Section	Row	Lot	Grave	

Oral History Interviews

Family Surname:

_____

Interviewing family members provides some of the most riveting information about your family. With the collected information, you have the basis for specific questions to ask family and friends to uncover more information.

The Resources section provides information on interviewing family members and friends, as well as sample question sources.

Review the sample questions listed for each section and include your own questions (if necessary). When interviewing your relative, write their responses in the space provided.

Date of Interview:

Location of Interview:

Interviewer:

Interviewee:

Relation Between Interviewer and Interviewee:

Tips

* Record the date and location of the interview, as well as the names of the interviewer and the interviewee.

* Use a recording app on your phone, or bring a tape recorder, to record the session. Please note: If you plan to use a digital device to record your interview session, make sure you have your interview subject's permission.

* Don't be afraid to let your interviewee talk "off subject." Some of the best stories happen when family members reminisce or share additional events or occurrences.

* Always take handwritten notes during the course of the interview.

* Don't push your family members for answers. They may be uncomfortable answering a question that may seem straightforward to you.

* Don't become frustrated if your family member can't remember specifics, like dates and times something occurred. Instead, you can ask if an event or occurrence happened before or after a significant event in the family.

Early Childhood and Family Background

Sample Questions
- Who did you grow up with in your household?
- How did your family celebrate holidays, birthdays, and wedding anniversaries?
- What fun activities did you do with your friends?

Teenage Years

Sample Questions
- What was your social life like?
- What life plans did you have when you were a teenager?
- What were the changes in the family when you were a teenager?

Adulthood

Sample Questions
- Did you continue your education? If so, where, when, and what did you study?
- Where did you live? What was that place like?
- How many times did you move? Where did you live?

Family Lore and Stories

Sample Questions
- What rumors have you heard about earlier family members?
- What celebrities have you met? Do you know of anyone else in the family who has?
- Have you, or has anyone else in the family, ever won a sports championship or a contest?

War Stories and Immigration Stories

Sample Questions
- When was your military service?
- What was your battalion's name?
- Where were you stationed?

Oral History Interview Tracker

Interviewer:

Date of Interview:

As you interview people about family members, you will want to have a handy list of people you have interviewed. The Oral History Interview Tracker lets you note with whom you have spoken, when you spoke with them, how long the interview lasted, as well as providing spaces for you to add where you have stored your interview files.

Family Surname:

_____

Name of the ancestor who is the subject of the interview:

_____

Notes:

Family Reference Number:_____

Interviews

No.	Name	Date	Duration	Method *(audio, video, written)*	Consent Given? *(Y or N)*	Name of Media File	Media File Storage Location
1							
2							
3							
4							
5							
6							
7							
8							
9							
10							

Family Photo Log

Family Surname:

_____

Organizing hundreds of photos, slides, and negatives that have been passed down through generations can be overwhelming. Tackle this task in a logical, streamlined manner. For example, organizing by major categories is a good place to start. The way you organize your family photo collection will depend on what is convenient and sensible for you.

Collection Name (family surname)	# of photos

Family Heirloom Log

Family Surname:

_____

This worksheet tracks the basic information about your family's heirlooms: who owns them, and who is next in line to receive them. There is space to provide a description for each heirloom. Consider taking pictures of the heirlooms you list and compiling them in a separate folder.

Heirloom	Heirloom Description

Collection Description (Smith family holiday photos)	Time Period Covered (1970-1990)	Primary Place Photos Were Taken	Location of Stored Photos	Location of Digital Photos

Is There a Story Attached to the Heirloom? What Is Its History?	Person Who Currently Owns the Heirloom	When and How Did Current Owner Come to Possess It?	Current Owner's Contact Information	Who Will Receive the Heirloom Next?

DNA Tracker

DNA testing has exploded as a popular pastime in America and can be one of the key methods you use to find your biological relations. Research shows more than 26 million people have taken an at-home ancestry test, according to MIT *Technology Review* (February 2016).

The series of DNA-related worksheets that follow are for people who have taken a DNA test with some of the major commercial DNA testing companies. There are additional worksheets for those who are interested in uploading their DNA test results from free DNA analysis services.

Familiarize yourself with the five DNA-related terms below before you begin working with the worksheets:

AUTOSOMAL (ATDNA) DNA is passed down randomly from generation to generation. A child does not inherit his or her parents' entire genetic makeup.

CENTIMORGAN (cM) is a DNA unit of measure that tells you how much DNA you share with another match. The more DNA you share with a match, the higher the cM number, and the more closely related you are to a DNA match.

HAPLOGROUP is a genetic population group of people who share a common ancestor on a patriline (male-to-male ancestral lineage) or the matriline (female-to-female ancestral lineage).

MITOCHONDRIAL DNA (MTDNA) is a genealogical DNA test used to explore a woman's matrilineal, or direct female-to-female-line ancestry.

Y-DNA is a genealogical DNA test used to explore a man's patrilineal, or direct male-to-male-line ancestry.

The worksheets are arranged by a central theme to help guide and instruct you to successfully add your information and support you as you begin to analyze your DNA test results.

Refer to the Resources section for a comprehensive list of DNA-related resources to guide you through the different aspects of working with DNA match results.

Family DNA Test Summary

Family Surname:_____

This part of the DNA tracker worksheet series enables you to summarize your DNA test results from different DNA testing services, if you have tested with more than one DNA testing service.

➡ Work your way from left to right. Begin by adding your name and DNA Test Service information to the "Your DNA Summary" section.

➡ Complete the details for the paternal side of your family in the "Your Father's Family" section.

➡ Complete the details for the maternal side of your family in the "Your Mother's Family" section.

Your DNA Summary

Your Name:	MyHeritage User ID:
Ancestry Username:	GEDmatch Kit ID:
23andMe User ID:	Y-DNA Haplogroup and Subclade: (*or your father's Y-DNA if you are female*)
FamilyTreeDNA (FTDNA) User ID:	
	mtDNA Haplogroup and Subclade:

Your Father's Family

Father's Name	Paternal Grandfather's Name	Paternal Grandmother's Name
Ancestry Username:	Ancestry Username:	Ancestry Username:
23andMe User ID:	23andMe User ID:	23andMe User ID:
FamilyTreeDNA (FTDNA) User ID:	FamilyTreeDNA (FTDNA) User ID:	FamilyTreeDNA (FTDNA) User ID:
MyHeritage User ID:	MyHeritage User ID:	MyHeritage User ID:
GEDmatch Kit ID:	GEDmatch Kit ID:	GEDmatch Kit ID:
Y-DNA Haplogroup and Subclade:	Y-DNA Haplogroup and Subclade:	Her father's Y-DNA Haplogroup and Subclade:
mtDNA Haplogroup and Subclade:	mtDNA Haplogroup and Subclade:	mtDNA Haplogroup and Subclade:

Your Mother's Family

Mother's Name	Maternal Grandfather's Name	Maternal Grandmother's Name
Ancestry Username:	Ancestry Username:	Ancestry Username:
23andMe User ID:	23andMe User ID:	23andMe User ID:
FamilyTreeDNA (FTDNA) User ID:	FamilyTreeDNA (FTDNA) User ID:	FamilyTreeDNA (FTDNA) User ID:
MyHeritage User ID:	MyHeritage User ID:	MyHeritage User ID:
GEDmatch Kit ID:	GEDmatch Kit ID:	GEDmatch Kit ID:
Her father's Y-DNA Haplogroup and Subclade:	Y-DNA Haplogroup and Subclade:	Her father's Y-DNA Haplogroup and Subclade:
mtDNA Haplogroup and Subclade:	mtDNA Haplogroup and Subclade:	mtDNA Haplogroup and Subclade:

DNA Notes

Cousin Chart

Family Surname:_____

Do you know the difference between a third cousin twice removed and a second cousin? It's easy to get into a muddle in sorting out different levels of cousinship when you're new to genealogy. The family relationship chart below displays family relationships over seven generations.

When it comes time to sort through hundreds, if not thousands, of DNA-test cousins, understanding how you and a newly discovered fourth cousin might be connected depends on you understanding at what generational level the two of you share a common ancestor. Different degrees of cousins will share different cM amounts. The amount of cMs you share with a DNA match can confirm what kind of cousin you are in relation to a DNA match. Explore the relationship between cMs and degree of cousinship in this worksheet.

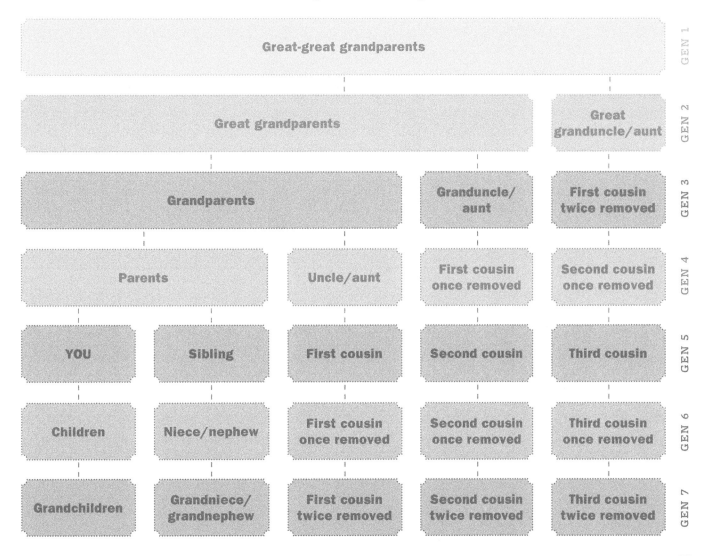

Family Relationships Chart

Family Surname:_____

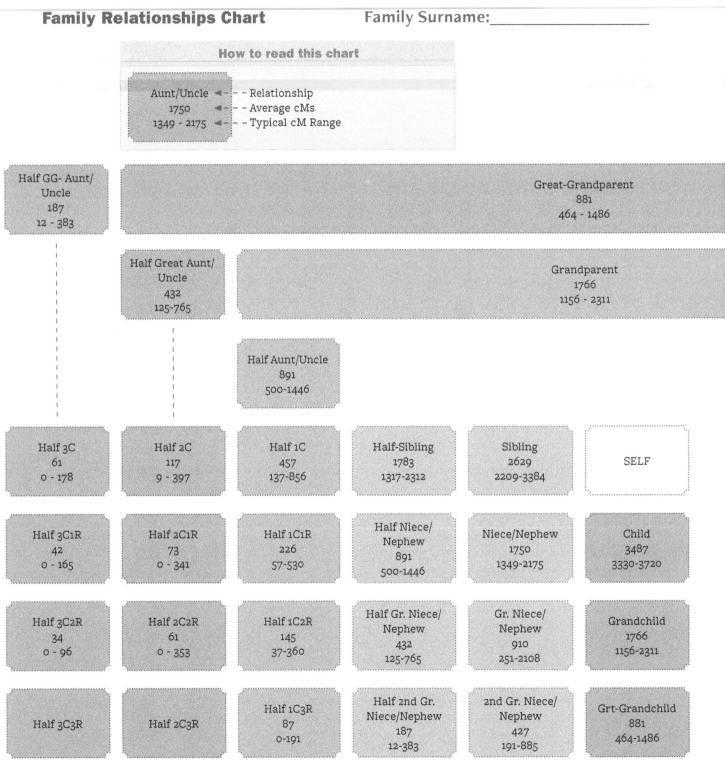

How to read this chart

Aunt/Uncle ◄---	-- Relationship
1750 ◄---	-- Average cMs
1349 - 2175 ◄---	-- Typical cM Range

Half GG- Aunt/Uncle 187 12 - 383				Great-Grandparent 881 464 - 1486
	Half Great Aunt/Uncle 432 125-765		Grandparent 1766 1156 - 2311	
		Half Aunt/Uncle 891 500-1446		

Half 3C 61 0 - 178	Half 2C 117 9 - 397	Half 1C 457 137-856	Half-Sibling 1783 1317-2312	Sibling 2629 2209-3384	SELF
Half 3C1R 42 0 - 165	Half 2C1R 73 0 - 341	Half 1C1R 226 57-530	Half Niece/Nephew 891 500-1446	Niece/Nephew 1750 1349-2175	Child 3487 3330-3720
Half 3C2R 34 0 - 96	Half 2C2R 61 0 - 353	Half 1C2R 145 37-360	Half Gr. Niece/Nephew 432 125-765	Gr. Niece/Nephew 910 251-2108	Grandchild 1766 1156-2311
Half 3C3R	Half 2C3R	Half 1C3R 87 0-191	Half 2nd Gr. Niece/Nephew 187 12-383	2nd Gr. Niece/Nephew 427 191-885	Grt-Grandchild 881 464-1486

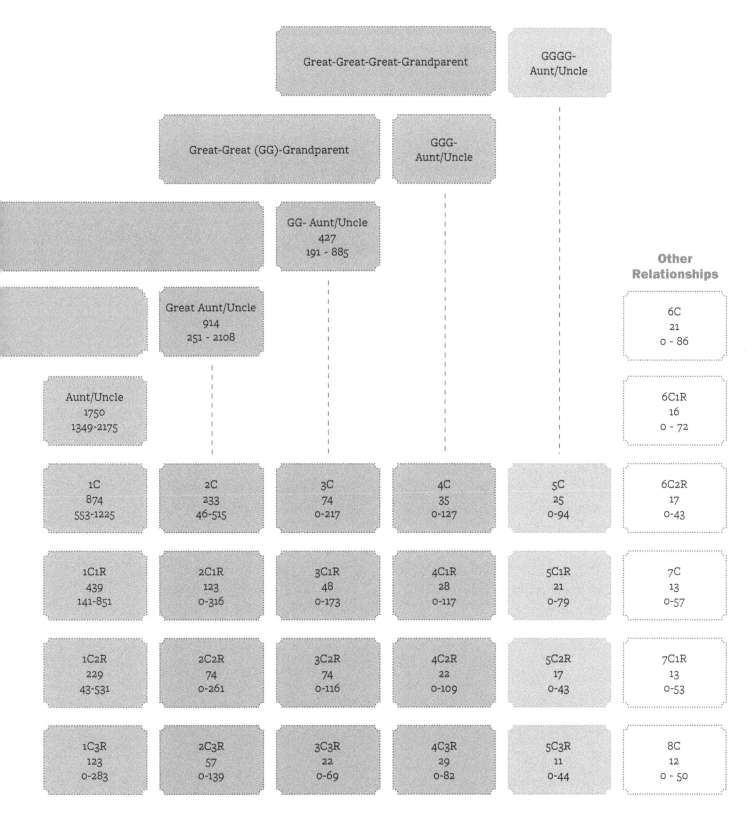

Great-Great-Great-Grandparent

GGGG-
Aunt/Uncle

Great-Great (GG)-Grandparent

GGG-
Aunt/Uncle

GG- Aunt/Uncle
427
191 - 885

Other Relationships

Great Aunt/Uncle
914
251 - 2108

6C
21
0 - 86

Aunt/Uncle
1750
1349-2175

6C1R
16
0 - 72

1C	2C	3C	4C	5C	6C2R
874	233	74	35	25	17
553-1225	46-515	0-217	0-127	0-94	0-43

1C1R	2C1R	3C1R	4C1R	5C1R	7C
439	123	48	28	21	13
141-851	0-316	0-173	0-117	0-79	0-57

1C2R	2C2R	3C2R	4C2R	5C2R	7C1R
229	74	74	22	17	13
43-531	0-261	0-116	0-109	0-43	0-53

1C3R	2C3R	3C3R	4C3R	5C3R	8C
123	57	22	29	11	12
0-283	0-139	0-69	0-82	0-44	0 - 50

Family Relationships Chart

Family Surname:_____

This worksheet has been provided for you to work with your DNA matches from a variety of DNA testing service providers. You will want to make many copies of this worksheet to support the DNA cousin matching research.

First, identify a DNA match that you would like to investigate in-depth and fill in the family tree that includes your line of descent and your DNA match's line of descent. Start with Box 1 (marked with a ☆). This is you, so put your name here. The box above this is for your mother or your father—the family line that links you to your DNA match. Continue filling in your direct ancestral line information back to your great grandparents. If you are managing someone else's DNA test, like one of your parents, enter their name in Box 1.

Next, add the details from your DNA match's tree. Their name and the cMs you share with them go into the bottom box at the same level as your name. Then add information about their ancestral line, starting with their parents. Spend some time to ensure that their genealogy is correct.

There is space for you to add information for four of your DNA matches who share a common ancestry with you and each other.

DNA Test Service Provider

(please check one)

Ancestry	
23andMe	
Family Tree DNA	
MyHeritage	
GEDmatch	

DNA Notes

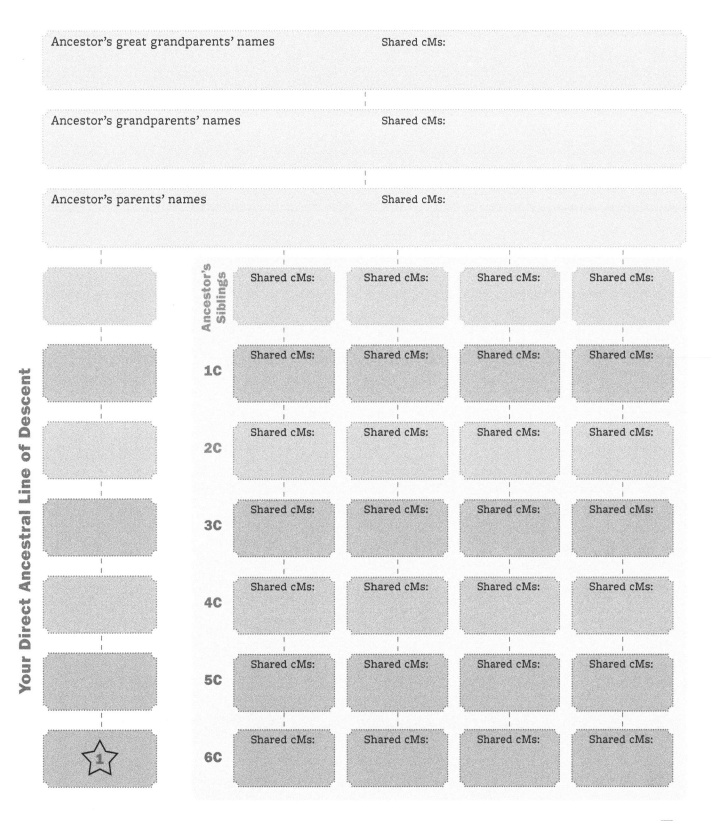

Ancestor's great grandparents' names   Shared cMs:

Ancestor's grandparents' names   Shared cMs:

Ancestor's parents' names   Shared cMs:

Your Direct Ancestral Line of Descent

Ancestor's Siblings

	Shared cMs:	Shared cMs:	Shared cMs:	Shared cMs:
1C	Shared cMs:	Shared cMs:	Shared cMs:	Shared cMs:
2C	Shared cMs:	Shared cMs:	Shared cMs:	Shared cMs:
3C	Shared cMs:	Shared cMs:	Shared cMs:	Shared cMs:
4C	Shared cMs:	Shared cMs:	Shared cMs:	Shared cMs:
5C	Shared cMs:	Shared cMs:	Shared cMs:	Shared cMs:
6C	Shared cMs:	Shared cMs:	Shared cMs:	Shared cMs:

1

In the News:
Newspaper Tracker

Family Surname:

_____

Old newspaper articles are a great way to discover more about an ancestor—as well as uncover some from family history golden nuggets. Start by looking at your pedigree chart. Identify information gaps that you might answer through newspaper articles, which can include engagement and marriage announcements. Start your newspaper search with a specific question to ensure that your research has a focus. Your research log is one place to add details about your discoveries; however, you can also add discoveries to the newspaper log.

Ancestor (with Family Ref. #)	Name of Newspaper	Newspaper Article Date	Date of Incident or Event

County & State Where Incident or Event Occurred	What Was the Article About?	Other Family Members Referenced? Who?	Newspaper Source Name (e.g., Newspapers.com)	Repository (add link if it was online or full address if it was microfilm)	Was There a Picture in the Article? (If so, location of where you saved it)

Free People of Color
Court Registration Log

Family Surname:

_____

African Americans who were legally free in the slavery era of American history were required to register with county courts to secure certificates of freedom, also known as freedom papers. Freedom papers and certificates of freedom were legal documents that declared the free status of black and mulatto people.

Freedom papers typically detail why the person involved had the status of a free man or a free woman of color. It could be that a previous enslaver freed them through a legal process known as manumission. The individuals may have been born to a free woman of color or a woman from a European background, which was noted on their freedom papers.

Freedom papers also contain an affidavit from a witness, who was typically a trusted member of the community with a European background. Note that name. The witness could be a neighbor of the person who obtained the freedom papers and someone with whom your ancestor conducted business. If the witness and the free man or woman shared the same surname, there may be a family connection between the two, especially if the free person noted in the certificate was a mulatto, or a person of mixed European, African, or Native American ancestry.

While freedom papers typically were written with short paragraphs, those paragraphs can be packed with vital information for your family tree research.

Ancestor (with Family Ref #)	Registration Document Reference #

Registration State	Registration County	Registration Date	Description of Ancestor	Original Document Source	Original Document Location	Location of Your Saved Digital Copy

Sale of Enslaved People Deed Log

Family Surname:

_____

Researching enslaved people in America is challenging—but not impossible. The sense of achievement you will experience in reconnecting branches of your enslaved family that were disrupted and lost through slavery, is one of the most powerful and evocative experiences you will have in your genealogical research.

> Slave deed research will form a substantial part of the research you will undertake to document the lives of your enslaved African American ancestors. Deeds for the enslaved will cover the transfer of your enslaved ancestor from one enslaving family member to another, as well as their sale to third parties outside of their original enslaving family.

Accessing this specific set of deeds reveals the history of enslavement for ancestors as they were passed from family member to family member during their enslaved lives. Such deeds also document an ancestor leaving the family who first enslaved them to a different family.

Pay attention to all the enslaved people's names cited in a slave deed. Chances are, your ancestors were sold with a family member. The nature of the relationship between the enslaved people listed in a sales deed will require further research if the nature of that relationship isn't made clear on the deed. However, in many cases, the relationship between a child, or children, and at least one parent is clearly stated, thus providing invaluable historical information for genealogists.

Enslaved Person's Name	Description	Age at Time of Sale (if given)
Moses	Mulatto boy	Unknown

Estimated Birth Year (year of sale-age)	Name of Enslaver at the Time of Sale	New Enslaver's Name (sold to)	Deed State and County	Date Bought	Value/Sale Price	Location of Original Deed	Location of Your Saved Digital File
	Matthews, Solomon	Pope, Martin	Edgefield, South Carolina	12 Dec 1812	$800	Edgefield County Deeds, Box #1, Package 13	C:/Documents/ Williams-Family/Moses-Williams/ Deed15-1812.jpg

Enslavers' Estate Inventory:
Dispersal of Enslaved People Log

Family Surname:

Enslavers' probate records are an invaluable resource for African Americans researching their enslaved ancestors. The death of an enslaver was a key point in an enslaved person's life. This is one of the crucial points in time when enslaved families were split apart—regardless of whether they were passed individually to different family members or sold away outside of the enslaving family to different enslavers.

Inventories are key documents that researchers need to prove who enslaved an ancestor. Before 1865, a slaveholder's estate inventory includes their enslaved property. Enslavers' inventories are all the more important if an enslaver died intestate, or without a will. Concerning intestate estates, an estate inventory will be the only main document citing enslaved people at the time of an enslaver's death.

An inventory is a legal report of the property of the deceased person. This type of legal document calculates the value of the estate, including enslaved people, who were legally classified as property. Estate inventories are housed in county-level and state archives, as well as specialists' archives such as archives managed by genealogical and historical societies, museums, and university archives.

Some inventories include only the names and values of slaves. This makes it difficult, if not impossible, to discern family groups. For inventories that don't provide ages for the enslaved, it is possible to use their assessed value to estimate an age range. Some inventories suggest enslaved family units. Pay particular attention to women of childbearing age who are followed by children on an inventory. Note: Larger farms/plantations will have more than one enslaved person with the same name. Do not assume that all these names were related to one another.

Enslaved Person's Name	Description
Moses	Mulatto boy

Enslaver's Name: Date of Will:

Probate Date: Date of Dispersal of Enslaved People (if known):

Age at Time of Sale *(if given)*	Estimated Birth Year *(year of sale-age)*	Name of Enslaver at the Time of Sale	New Enslaver's Name *(sold to)*	Inventory State and County	Inventory Date	Value/ Sale Price	Location of Original Deed	Location of Your Saved Digital File
Unknown		Matthews, Solomon	Pope, Martin	Edgefield, South Carolina	12 Dec 1812	$800	Edgefield County Deeds, Box #1, Package 13	C:/Documents/ Williams- Family/Moses- Williams/ Deed15-1812.jpg

Enslavers' Wills: Dispersal of Enslaved People Log

Family Surname:

_____

Just like enslavers' estate inventories, wills are crucial documents that researchers need to find their enslaved ancestors and families. Like inventories, most wills will include the names of enslaved people who were bequeathed to family members within an enslaving family. Finding names might be difficult due to various ways that the identities of enslaved people were recorded. Refer to Worksheet 25: Enslavers' Estate Inventory: Dispersal of Enslaved People Log (page 66) for guidance on how to interpret enslaved family relationships when none have been provided in a probate document.

Enslaver's Name:

Date of Will:

Probate Date:

Enslaved Person's Name	If Listed with Family Members, add their Names in This Column
Davy	With wife, Sophy and children: Tobe, Alonza, Georgianna, Rachel, and Peter

New Enslaver's Name *(sold to)*	State and County Where Will Was Filed	Location of Original Will	Location of Your Saved Digital File
Richardson, Hezekiah	Charles City County, Virginia	Charles City County Order Book, 1694–1700, image 57	C:/Documents/Price-Family/Davy-Price/ John-Price-1699Will. docx

Eastern Cherokee Application: Family Sheet Log

Family Surname:

_____

The Eastern Cherokee Applications record collection at Fold3 contains applications from people who submitted their ancestral information to prove they were members of the Eastern and Western Cherokee. The basis for creating the Eastern Cherokee Application was a lawsuit brought by Eastern Cherokees who sued the United States for funds due to them under the treaties of 1835, 1836, and 1845.

The accompanying worksheet lets you note and log details that an ancestor provided in the Eastern Cherokee Application form. While the forms contain genealogical data, you will need to research further to ensure that the information is factually correct.

© *indicate both English and Native American names*

Ancestor's Name:

Application #:

Application Date:

Application Received:

Action / Application Decision *(Was the person admitted or denied?)*:

Ancestor and Their Household

Ancestor's English Name:

Ancestor's Native American Name:

Ancestor's Date of Birth:

Ancestor's Place of Birth:

Ancestor's Residential Street Address:

County:

State:

Spouse's Name:

Name of Children:

Rights to Claim

By what right did your ancestor make his or her claim? *(This is usually found at the front of the application)*

Ancestor's Parents

Father's Name:

Father's Place of Birth:

Father's Date of Death:

Mother's Name: *Use maiden name only*

Mother's Place of Birth:

Mother's Date of Death:

Parents' Residence in 1851:

Ancestor's Siblings

Name of Sibling	Sibling's Place of Birth	Sibling's Date of Death	Sibling's Place of Death

CONTINUED ON NEXT PAGE

Ancestor's Grandparents

○ Paternal Grandfather Name: | Place of Birth:

○ Paternal Grandmother Name: | Place of Birth:

○ Maternal Grandfather Name: | Place of Birth:

○ Maternal Grandmother Name: | Place of Birth:

Ancestor's Grandparents' Other Children

○ Name of Child	Child's Place of Birth	Child's Date of Death	Child's Place of Death

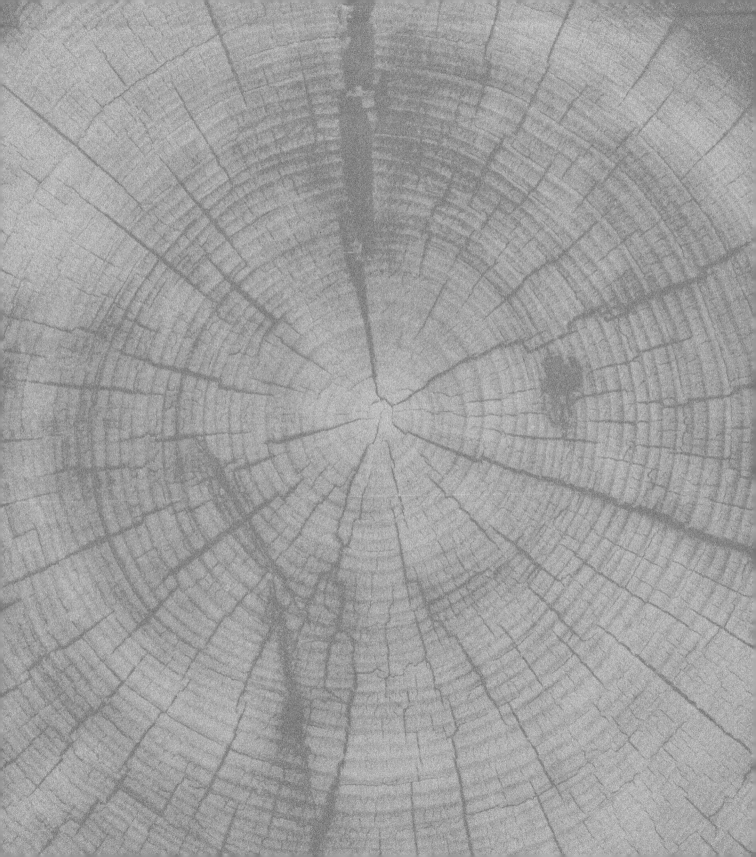

Dawes Enrollment Cards
Family Sheet Log

Family Surname:

The Dawes Enrollment Cards are a census-like listing for members of five Native American tribes, 1898–1914. The Dawes Commission created enrollment cards to record information about family groups within the Cherokee, Choctaw, Creek, Chickasaw, and Seminole nations. They list family relationships, degree of native blood, age, tribal enrollment, and other data useful to establishing family connections and Native American ancestry.

Dawes' Roll #	Name	Relationship to Person First Named	Age	Sex	Blood	Tribal Enrollment		
						Year	District	No:

Native American Tribal Nation Name:

Dawes Enrollment Card Number:

Field Number:

Residence:

Post Office:

Tribal Enrollment of Parents					
Name of Father	Year	District	Name of Mother	Year	District

PART 3

Census Information

A census record can tell you not only where and when your ancestor lived, but can also describe their occupation, other members of their household, and even small details about their life, such as previous military service or whether they owned a radio set.

The census has been taken every 10 years since the early days of the United States of America. They are used to reapportion seats in the House of Representatives, realign congressional districts, and factor into the formulas used to distribute hundreds of billions of dollars in federal funds each year. Because of the importance of this population count, procedural changes in the decennial census often reflect larger organizational shifts at the Census Bureau—and mean each decennial census form may look different.

U.S. Federal Census Questions at a Glance

Family Surname:

_____

The first U.S. Census began in 1790 and has been held every ten years to the present day. At the time of writing, the last publicly available census to research online is the 1940 Census. Due to privacy laws, census records are not available to the public until 72 years after the census date. With this 72-year rule in mind, the 1950 U.S. Census won't be available until April 2022.

These seemingly bland-looking forms can pack quite a punch when it comes to providing superb background information about people and the communities where they lived. They can also tell you quite a bit about your family, too!

One census year is mostly missing: the 1890 Census. Due to a fire that destroyed the location where the 1890 Census was stored, only fragments remain for this year.

The two census-related worksheets here reflect the changing nature of the U.S. Census records. Both census worksheets are designed for you to enter the information you glean for each census decade that is relevant to the ancestor you are researching.

See a full list of Census Records at https://www.archives.gov/research/census.

State:	1820 Federal Census											Microfilm Series:	
County or Parish:	Township/Town/Or City:											Date of Enumeration:	
		Free White Males						Free White females					
Page	Head of Family	Free white males under ten years	Free white males of ten and under sixteen	Free white males between sixteen and eighteen	Free white males of sixteen and under twenty-six, including heads of families	Free white males of twenty-six and under forty-five, including heads of families	Free white males of forty-five and upwards, including heads of families	Free white females under ten years	Free white females of ten and under sixteen	Free white females of sixteen and under twenty-six, including heads of families	Free white females of twenty-six and under forty-five, including heads of families	Free white females of forty-five and upwards, including heads of families
		to 10	10 to 15	16 to 18	16 to 25	26 to 44	45 & up	to 10	10 to 15	16 to 25	26 to 44	45 & up

The 1820 Census is just one example to take into account as you fill out the following Individual Census Checklist. Take note of the questions asked during this census, as opposed to others that come before and after.

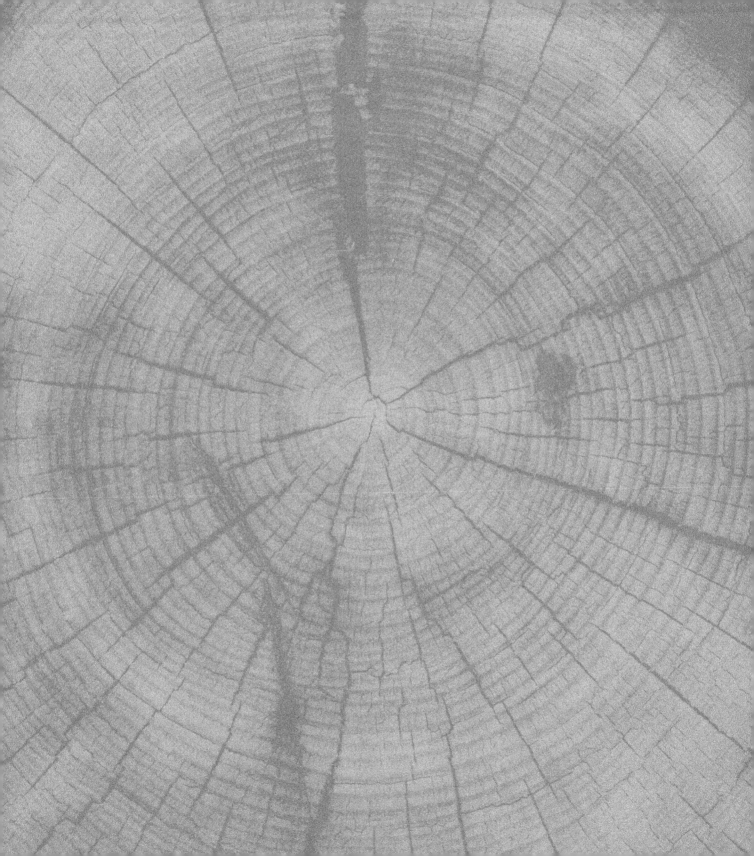

Individual Census Checklist

Family Surname:

_____

You have spent some time familiarizing yourself with how the information captured by census enumerators changed from decade to decade. Now it's time for you to start capturing and logging details you have discovered from your family's census records.

The accompanying worksheet provides you with space to record, preserve, and archive the family history data you discover from U.S. Census records. Make a copy of the blank worksheet. This is a worksheet you will wish to use and re-use in your research.

U.S. Federal Census Summary

Census Data for:	
Date of Birth:	
Date of Death:	
Married to:	

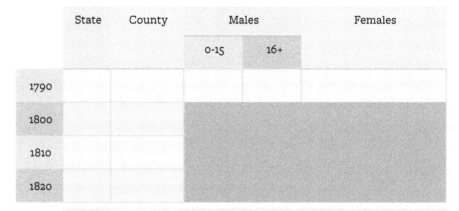

	State	County	Males		Females
			0-15	16+	
1790					
1800					
1810					
1820					

	State	County	Males									
			0-4	5-9	10-14	15-19	20-29	30-39	40-49	50-59	60-69	70-79
1830												
1840												

Name of person				Age	
Name of person				Age	
Name of person				Age	

	Name of person	State	County	Township	Age	Sex
1850						

Place of Birth:

Place of Death:

Marriage Date:

	Males					Females				Remarks
0-9	10-15	16-25	26-44	45+	0-9	10-15	16-25	26-44	45+	

Males			Females													Remarks
80-89	90-99	100+	0-4	5-9	10-14	15-19	20-29	30-39	40-49	50-59	60-69	70-79	80-89	90-99	100+	

Name of person	Age
Name of person	Age
Name of person	Age

Occupation	Birthplace	Married within year	Remarks

CONTINUED ON NEXT PAGE

	Name of person	State	County	Township	Age	Sex
1860						
1870						

	Name of person	State	County	Township	Age	Sex
1880						

	Name of person	State	County	Township	Relation to head
1900					

Occupation	Birthplace	Married within year	Remarks

CONTINUED ON NEXT PAGE

Relation to head	Marital status	Occupation	Birthplace		
			Person	Father	Mother

Sex	DOB		Marital status	Birthplace			Year nat.	Years in U.S.
	Month	Year		Person	Father	Mother		

	Name of person	State	County	Township	Relation to head
1910					

	Name of person	State	County	Township	Relation to head
1920					
1930					
1940					

Sex	Age	Marriage		Children			Birthplace			Year of immig.	Nat.
		Status	Years	Born	Living	Person	Father	Mother			

Sex	Age	Marital status	Year of immig.	Year nat.	Birthplace		
					Person	Father	Mother

Passenger Arrival Record

Family Surname:

_____

Passenger arrival records can be a useful resource when it comes to researching immigrant ancestors. Arrival records can provide a wealth of information, including:

➤ the nationality and place of birth for the person or persons who arrived in the U.S.;

➤ name of the ship;

➤ date of entry to the U.S.;

➤ age, height, eye and hair color;

➤ profession or occupation;

➤ place of last residence;

➤ name(s) of relatives with whom they traveled;

➤ date of arrival; and

➤ name and address of relatives the arrivals were joining in the U.S.

The accompanying worksheet helps you to capture and save information about your ancestors who arrived by ship.

Passenger Number on List	Name In Full		Age		If more than 1 family member in group, what is the relationship between them?	Gender (Sex)	Married or Single	Occupation
	Family Name	Given Name	Years	Months				

| Physical Description | Able to | | | Nationality (Country of which citizen or subject) | Race or people | Last permanent address | | The name and complete address of nearest relative or friend in country whence alien came | Final destination | | U.S. Family or Friend (who are they staying with?) | |
	Read	Read what language	Write			Country	City or town		State	City or town	Family member or Friend	Host Family/ Friend Address

PART 4

Managing Information

Your online searches and in-person visits to secure the documents and records you need to support your research will result in hundreds, if not thousands, of paper and digital records. Keeping track of all the materials you have gathered is paramount. The organization of these materials is the key to keeping your research materials and discoveries accessible, safe, and manageable. The guidance in this section will help you keep your hard work in order and your research on-track—setting you up for success.

Research Checklist

Family Surname:

_____

Ancestor's Name
(*include Family Ref. #*):

_____

As you add more family members to your family tree, how can you possibly remember what research you have done for each person? A research checklist acts like an inventory for your research sources and materials. In a glance, it will tell you the records and documents you have found and saved and those that remain to be discovered and used.

Another benefit of a checklist is that it will jog your memory for details you may have forgotten, or information you have missed, which can influence your research and findings. Have you really thought of every resource that can answer the question of where your fourth great grandmother was born? A checklist will immediately show you.

The checklist here is something you can quickly return to and reference. Keeping it up-to-date will ensure you have covered all bases and located the necessary information sources during the research process.

Names (with Family Ref. #)	Birth Record	Marriage Records	Death Certificate	Funeral Program	Obituary	Letters / Diary	Land / Property Records

Items Around the House

Notes

School Records	Legal Records	Religious Records	Health Records	Government Records	Family Bible	Family Photographs	Insurance Policies	Immigration / Naturalization Records	Business Records	Travel Records / Passport

CONTINUED ON NEXT PAGE

Notes

Names (with Family Ref. #)	Outside Sources								
	Local Archives	State Archives	University Archives	Genealogical & Historical Socities	Local & Regional Libraries	State Library	Private Libraries	Churches	Family History Centers

Outside Records & Information

Cemeteries	Tax Records	Military Records	Legal Records / Court Cases / Court Documents	Probate Records	Land Records	Birth Records	Marriage Records	U.S. Census Records & Schedules	Death Records / Mortality Schedule	Deeds	City Directories	Family & Friends Interviews	Immigration & Naturalization Records	Online Databases	Local / Regional Historical Books	Newspapers	Websites

Worksheet Index

Family Surname:

_____

To support your organization efforts, this Worksheet Index helps you track the worksheets you have used to document an ancestor. Think of this index as a master list of worksheets you have used to log information for an ancestor.

Ancestor:			
Worksheets			
Pedigree Chart:		Oral History Interviews Tracker:	
Ancestor Overview Worksheet:		Family Photo Log:	
Ancestor Overview Worksheet—Part 1 (Paternal Pedigree)		Family Heirloom Log:	
Ancestor Overview Worksheet—Part 2 (Maternal Pedigree)		DNA Tracker:	
Family Address Worksheet:		In the News: Newspaper Tracker	
Family Group Worksheet:		Free People of Color Court Registration Log:	
Sibling Worksheet:		Sale of Enslaved People Deed Log:	
Blended Family Worksheet:		Enslavers' Estate Inventory: Dispersal of Enslaved People Log:	
Family Group Timeline:		Enslavers' Wills: Dispersal of Enslaved People Log:	
U.S. Family Migration Map:		Eastern Cherokee Application: Family Sheet Log:	
World Family Migration Map:		Dawes Enrollment Cards Family Sheet Log:	
Marriage Records:		U.S. Federal Census Questions at a Glance (1790-1940)	
Land Deed Index:		Individual Census Checklist:	
Military History Checklist:		Passenger Arrival Record:	
Military Service Log:		Research Checklist:	
Family Medical History:		Worksheet Index:	
Death Record Search Log:		Source Documentation List:	
Cemetery Research Log:		15 Things to Do When You're Stumped:	
Oral History Interviews:		Future Proofing Your Genealogy Research:	

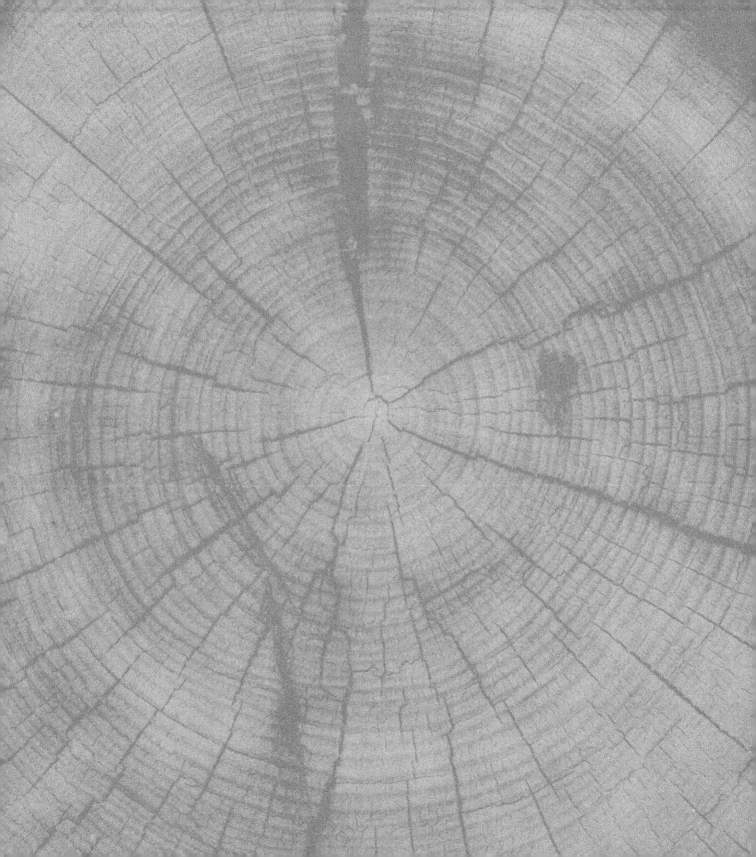

Source Documentation List

Family Surname:

_____

S ource Documentation Lists provide a single place to identify a master reference list for genealogical-related documentation and records that represent your collected knowledge.

The following Source Documentation List allows you to log and track all of the sources you have used during the process of researching an ancestor and their family.

Author(s)	Article Title or Book Title, or Website Name	Publisher's Information			
		Publisher	Pub. Date	Call #	Vol. # and Page #

	Resource Search					Notes
Location of Repository, Database, or Website	I Have This Resource?	I Need This Resource?	Where Did I Look for This Resource?	How Did I Search to Find This Resource (e.g., search keywords)	Worksheets This Information Has Been Added To	Including Other Search Strategies to Try

PART 5

Reaching Completion

A genealogist's work is never truly finished. Family research is ongoing, and a work in progress. The sense of connection you will develop with a long-deceased ancestor is the power of genealogy. It is a personally transformative experience. While you may never discover every aspect of ancestors' lives, what you do uncover and learn about them should give you a sense of accomplishment.

It is also good practice to revisit family research for a specific family line every three to five years. Think about how your research journey began and what you have accomplished at the end of researching an ancestor. You won't be the same person. New researchers are typically filled with doubt, but continue to persevere and you will build the confidence you need to succeed.

15 Things to Do When You Are Stumped

Getting stumped about an ancestor's life is part of genealogical research. Some ancestors are difficult to research due to a scarcity of records for or about them. Think of this like a crime scene investigator. Sometimes, all you will have to work with is a partial fingerprint. A partial print is better than no fingerprint at all.

> Sometimes, researchers get stumped because of inaccuracies and inconsistencies in the information they have gathered. Alternatively, your research may come to a screeching halt because you've missed information that you overlooked in a record, or you may have applied the wrong record, like a death certificate, to an incorrect person in your tree.

Never fear. There are work-arounds and methodologies when it comes to succeeding in your research when all seems lost:

1 Account for Inconsistencies

Be forthright about discrepancies you have uncovered in your research to strengthen your ability to interpret evidence.

2 Explain Name Variations

Name misspellings are common in genealogy-related records. As you build your tree, pay attention to how different lines from the same family may have spelled their surname differently. Try to search using name variations.

3 Recognize Patterns

Family naming patterns are often overlooked clues. Some first names often repeat down the generations within a single family's ancestral line. Middle names are also important, especially if the middle name in question is a surname.

4 Find Family Stories in Newspapers

Newspapers are a great resource for finding details about births, marriages, deaths, property transactions, business affairs, political affairs, and other community news that may have involved an ancestor.

5 Other Printed Resources

Newsletters, school and university student and alumni lists and profiles, military academy yearbooks, church newsletters or meeting minutes, and community pamphlets are valuable resources. You may find birth, marriage, and religious community announcements, obituaries, oral histories, and more that can fill in gaps in your research.

6 Search for Ancestors' Siblings

You can break through some stubborn brick walls by researching an ancestor's siblings.

7 Search Family History Publications and Genealogical Journals

Family history publications and genealogical journals can include record abstracts and published family sketches. These articles demonstrate techniques you can apply to your own research. They also contain trusted sources you can use in your research.

8 Locate the Original Record

Chances are you will come across a transcription, or written abstract, of an original document. Original records can provide additional information in the form of handwritten notes in the margins or on the back of the original.

9 Find a Local Historical or Genealogical Society or a Genealogy Library

Local historical and genealogical societies and genealogy libraries offer a wealth of resources for genealogy researchers, as do local public libraries. You may also find a local volunteer who can assist you in your research.

10 Think Outside the Record Set

You cannot access all records online. Many genealogy-related records are available offline at libraries and archives. Manuscript collections, for instance, can be a research goldmine.

11 Location, Location, Location—and Maps

Be sure to investigate possible variations of place names. Maps can play an important role. Note that boundaries over the years can change, so take this into consideration.

12 Locations Again: Look Around

An ancestor may have lived in one place, yet filed paperwork in another location. If your ancestor is associated with more than one place, search for records in each place with which they were associated.

13 Reach Out to Other Researchers

Another option you can use to break through brick walls is leaving your name, the surname you are researching, and your contact information on online genealogy research groups, forums, and bulletin boards.

14 Participate in a DNA Study

DNA testing and analysis can achieve powerful results. You can participate in DNA surname studies, which combine genealogical research and DNA results. You may also work with your DNA results to identify parents and siblings for an ancestor who is proving difficult to research.

15 Attend a Webinar, Class, or Genealogy Conference and Seminar

Your local area may have opportunities to learn more about researching your family. These tutorial sessions can either be online or in a local venue like a library.

Future-Proofing Your Genealogy Research

Once you've been bitten by the genealogy bug, it becomes a lifelong vocation. Along the way, you will accumulate an unimaginable number of stories, photographs, documents and records, books, and a multitude of other memorabilia. Until science figures out a way for us to live forever, what will become of all your hard research work and materials you gathered?

You'll need to organize your genealogical affairs. This section provides some practical advice to ensure that the next generation of researchers can benefit from your years of dedication and hard work.

Create a Research Inventory

The first step in future-proofing your research is documenting your research, and the materials you have collected during your research. It's time to create an inventory of all your research items.

Digital Materials

You can save your digitized materials in a variety of ways. For instance, "the cloud" (e.g., Dropbox, OneDrive, Google Cloud), DVDs, flash drives, a backup tablet, and device or space where you can securely and safely store digitized files.

Materials that you can save on a device or in the cloud include:

➤ Digital books, magazines, newsletters, and newspaper clippings;

➤ Scanned photographs and documents;

➤ Digital documents like PDFs, as well as your research reports and blog posts;

➤ Emails; and

➤ Maps and land records.

Print and Hard Copy Materials

You can use a binder, notebook, this workbook, or a box folder to safely store the hard copy materials you have collected in your research. Ways to secure materials include:

➤ Genealogy magazines and newsletters;

➤ Genealogy research binders, folders, and loose papers;

- Photos, slides, videos, CDs, flash drives, and DVDs; and
- Additional items such as audio recordings.

Add a note or a label that you can attach to each binder, notebook, or box folder that you use to store your hard copy materials. This note or label should also have your instructions on what you would like to happen to the materials that it contains. This will let whoever is sorting through your possessions know your wishes in terms of disseminating your research materials.

Your Online Profiles

Working online is now an established part and parcel of genealogical research. Saving, sharing, and commenting on discoveries is an everyday occurrence on social media, websites, and apps. What can you do to ensure that the people you want to have access to your online spaces can actually access these online spaces?

Create a master document that lists the online spaces that you have created (e.g., blog, website, social media) and your login credentials. Print out your list of online spaces and keep it with estate planning papers. You can also store this list in a safe or locked drawer. Wherever you store it, let one or two trusted family members or friends know the list's location so they can access it when necessary.

Donate Your Research to Local Archives, Societies, and Libraries

If it isn't possible to hand your research over to a family member who is dedicated to continuing your research work, you might consider donating your research and materials to a local archive or historical or genealogical society, as well as a local library. Such organizations will have guidelines and policies about what materials they will receive. You will need to review an organization's donation policy to ensure that they will accept your collection and research.

GLOSSARY

ABSTRACT: An abbreviated transcription of a document that includes the date of the record and every name it contains; it may also provide relationships or descriptions (witness, executor, bondsman, son, widow) of the people mentioned.

AUTOSOMAL DNA: Genetic material inherited equally from both parents. It's less useful genealogically than Y-DNA and mtDNA because it mutates more often.

BLOCK NUMBER: A one-, two-, or three-digit number that describes a block (or piece) of land within a township.

BOND: A written, signed, and witnessed agreement requiring someone to pay a specified amount of money by a given date.

BONDSMAN: The person legally liable for the debt or default of another; they appear on early marriage bonds.

CERTIFIED COPY: A copy made and attested to by officers who are responsible for keeping the original record or document and who are authorized to give copies.

CHROMOSOME: A threadlike strand of DNA that carries genes and transmits hereditary information.

DECLARATION OF INTENTION: An alien's sworn statement that he or she wants to become a U.S. citizen, also called "first papers." These records, which were filed in federal court, list personal details such as name, age, occupation, birthplace, last foreign residence, and more.

DEED: A document transferring ownership and title of property. Unlike a patent, a deed records the sale of property from one private individual to another.

DEED BOOK: Books that contain a record of property transfers and other kinds of property sales within a county. Deed books are kept at a county courthouse and are usually under the jurisdiction of the Registrar of Deeds.

DEED REGISTRY: Also known as a registry of deeds. A deed registry is a record of real estate deeds or other land titles that a local government official maintains.

ENUMERATION DISTRICTS: Divisions of each county and some large cities used to make census taking more efficient and accurate. For large cities, the boundaries of enumeration districts often match those of wards or precincts.

FREEDMAN: Men and women who were freed from slavery: an emancipated person.

GRANTEE: A legal term used in real estate transactions. The grantee, or buyer, receives title to a piece of real estate.

GRANTOR: A legal term used in real estate transactions. The grantor is the seller of a property such as a house. The individual conveys or gives title to a grantee—the buyer. A grantor transfers title to a grantee through a legal instrument known as a deed.

INDEX: An alphabetical list of names from a particular set of records. For example, a census index lists the names of people from a particular set of census records, such as the 1870 or 1900 census. Indexes come in book form and on CDs, microfilm, and microfiche.

INTERNATIONAL GENEALOGICAL INDEX (IGI): The International Genealogical Index (IGI) is one of the resources of the Family History Library of the Church of Jesus Christ of Latter-day Saints. An index of people's names (around 250 million) that were either submitted to the church, or were extracted from records that the church has microfilmed over the years.

INTESTATE: Description of a person who died without leaving a will.

MANUSCRIPTS: Handwritten documents and records such as diaries, letters, or family Bible entries that can contain items relating to family, business, or organization papers. Find manuscript collections by consulting the National Union Catalog of Manuscript Collections (NUCMC), which shows libraries that keep manuscript documents.

MATRILINEAL ANCESTRY: Also referred to as a **MATERNAL LINE**. Matrilineality traces kinship through a female family line, or a person's mother's lineage. A matriline is a line of descent from a female ancestor to a descendant of either gender.

MIRACODE SYSTEM: An indexing system similar to Soundex that the U.S. government used to organize the 1910 Census results. Today, miracode index cards are computer generated rather than handwritten, and are organized first by Soundex code, then alphabetically by county, then alphabetically by given name.

MORTALITY SCHEDULE A section of the Federal Census listing information about persons who died during the census year.

NATIONAL ARCHIVES AND RECORDS ADMINISTRATION (NARA): The United States' archive of all federal records, including census records, military service rolls and pension applications, passenger lists, and bounty-land warrants. In addition to the primary archives in Washington, DC, NARA has 13 regional facilities across the nation.

PASSENGER LIST: List of the names and information about passengers who arrived on ships into the United States. The ship's master submitted these lists to customs collectors at every port.

PATRILINEAL ANCESTRY: Also referred to as a **PATERNAL LINE**. Patrilineality traces kinship through a male family line, or a person's father's lineage. A patriline is a line of descent from a male ancestor to a descendant of either gender.

PEDIGREE: A list of a person's ancestors.

PENSION (MILITARY): A benefit paid regularly to a veteran, or his widow, for military service or a military service-related disability.

PRIMARY SOURCE: A record or other source created at the time of a particular event. A primary source is always the original record. For example, birth and death certificates are primary sources for those events. An original record is not always a primary source. For example, a death certificate is not a primary source of birth information.

PROBATE RECORDS: Records disposing of a deceased individual's property. They may include an individual's last will and testament, if one was made, and an estate inventory, or a compilation of property at the time of death. The information you can obtain from probate records varies but usually includes the name of the deceased, either the deceased's age at the time of death or birth date, property, members of the family, and the last place of residence.

REAL PROPERTY: Land and anything attached to it, such as houses, buildings, barns, growing timber, and growing crops.

SECONDARY SOURCE: A record created after an event occurred, such as a biography, local history, index, oral history interview, or computer database. Original records also can be secondary sources for information about earlier events. For example, a marriage certificate would be a secondary source for a birth date because the birth took place several years before the time of the marriage. Use the details you find in secondary sources as clues until you can verify them in original records.

SOUNDEX: A system of coding surnames based on how they sound, which the U.S. government used to index the 1880 and later censuses. The Soundex system is useful in locating records containing alternate surname spellings. Soundex cards are arranged first by Soundex code, then alphabetically by given name, then (if necessary) alphabetically by place of birth.

VITAL RECORDS: The most basic information available for a person; these statistics—found in vital records—include birth (abbreviated b), marriage date and place (abbreviated m), divorce date and place if applicable (abbreviated div), and death date and burial place (abbreviated d and bur).

VOLUME NUMBER: On a Soundex or Miracode index card, the number of the census volume in which the indexed name appears.

WILL: A document in which people outline their estate wishes after death. The legal process to carry out those instructions is called probate.

WITNESS: A person who sees an event and signs a document attesting to its accuracy. Although family members often served as witnesses, do not assume that witnesses on a record are relatives. Friends, neighbors, and business associates also commonly witness documents.

Y CHROMOSOME: Genetic material passed down from father to son. Because surnames also pass from father to son, Y-DNA tests can confirm (or disprove) genealogical links through a paternal line. Y-DNA surname studies are the most popular application of genetic genealogy.

RESOURCES

Land and Land Deed Research

Durie, B. (2013). *Understanding Documents for Genealogy and Local History.* History Press Ltd.

Hone, E. W. (1997). *Land & Property Research in the United States.* Ancestry.com.

Thorndale, W. (1987). *Map Guide to the U.S. Federal Censuses, 1790-1920.* Baltimore: Genealogical Publishing Company.

Interviewing Family Members and Friends Resources

Ewell, B. (2014, February 11). "Genealogy: 150 Questions to Ask Family Members about Their Lives." *Deseret News.* Retrieved December 18, 2019, from www.deseret.com.

Hart, C. (2010). *The Oral History Workshop.* New York: Workman Publishing.

UCLA Library Services. (2015). "Family History Sample Outline and Questions." UCLA. Retrieved December 18, 2019, from oralhistory.library.ucla .edu/familyHistory.html.

Military Service History Research

(n.d.). "Research in Military Records." National Archives. Retrieved December 18, 2019, from www.archives.gov/research/military.

Huber, L. A. (2016). "Finding US Military Ancestors in Online Records." *FamilySearch Blog.* Retrieved December 18, 2019, from www.familysearch .org/blog.

Neagles, J. C. (1994). *U.S. Military Records.* Salt Lake City, Utah: Ancestry Publishing Company.

Death Record and Cemetery Research

Carmack, S. D. (2002). *Your Guide to Cemetery Research.* Cincinnati, Ohio: Betterway Books.

Keister, D. (2004). *Stories in Stone.* Gibbs Smith.

Leonard, B. (2007). *Where to Write for Vital Records.* DIANE Publishing.

DNA and Genetic Genealogy Research

Bettinger, B. T. (2016). *Genetic Genealogy in Practice.* National Genealogical Society.

Bettinger, B. T. (2016). *The Family Tree Guide to DNA Testing and Genetic Genealogy.* Family Tree Books.

Free People of Color Research

Berry, K. D. (2016). "Genealogy Tips: Researching Free People of Color." Retrieved December 18, 2019, from *Genealogy Roadshow* on PBS.

Heinegg, P. (2018). "Free African Americans of Virginia, North Carolina, South Carolina, Maryland and Delaware." Free African Americans. Retrieved December 18, 2019, from www.freeafricanamericans.com.

Enslaved Africans Research

Burroughs, T. (2001). *Black Roots: A Beginner's Guide to Tracing the African-American Family Tree.* Touchstone.

Eltis, D. (2015). *Atlas of the Transatlantic Slave Trade.* The Lewis Walpole Series in Eighteenth-Century Culture and History. Yale University Press.

Smith, F. C. (2009). *A Genealogist's Guide to Discovering Your African-American Ancestors.* Genealogical Publishing Company.

Native American Research

Ocean, S. (2014). *Native Americans Hidden in Our Family Trees* (Secret Genealogy #4). CreateSpace.

Passenger Arrival Research

Carmack, S. (2005). *The Family Tree Guide to Finding Your Ellis Island Ancestors.* Family Tree Books.

Colletta, J. P. (2002). *They Came in Ships.* Orem, Utah: Ancestry Publishing.

Eltis, D. (2015). *Atlas of the Transatlantic Slave Trade.* The Lewis Walpole Series in Eighteenth-Century Culture and History. Yale University Press.

Emory University (2010). "Slave Voyages." Emory Center for Digital Scholarship. Retrieved December 18, 2019, from www.slavevoyages.org.

Tepper, M. (1993). *American Passenger Arrival Records.* Baltimore: Genealogical Publishing Company.

REFERENCES

(n.d.). (1981). "Eastern Cherokee Applications of the U.S. Court of Claims 1906-1919." National Archives Trust Fund Board, National Archives and Records Service.

Booker, C. (2006). *The Seven Basic Plots.* A&C Black.

Carmack, S. D. (2000). *Bringing Your Family History to Life Through Social History.* North Light Books.

Regalado, A. (2019). "More Than 26 Million People Have Taken an At-Home Ancestry Test." *MIT Technology Review.* 11 February 2019. Last accessed: 9 December 2019.

Stareva, I. (2015). "The 7 Best Storytelling Infographics You Need to Check Out Now." *Iliyana's Blog.* Retrieved December 30, 2019, from www.iliyanastareva.com/blog.

INDEX

ACKNOWLEDGMENTS

I stand on the shoulders of genealogical giants. While there are too many people to mention by name, the genealogists, librarians, local historians, public historians, history enthusiasts, academic researchers, truth seekers, and authors who have inspired my work and patiently explained important genealogy research strategies when I was new to genealogy: The time you have spent with me over the years will never be forgotten. I am in your debt.

I would like to thank FamilySearch and *Family Tree Magazine* for the exceptional genealogical research articles they publish and share online. The articles they publish provide critical genealogical research strategies and general research information. They were invaluable to me when I began my initial foray into the world of genealogy.

I also would also like to thank the extraordinarily talented Genealogy Adventures research team. You are all always there for me when the going gets tough, when I am faced with seemingly insurmountable research barriers, or when the stories I find along the way are too painful to bear alone. You are my strength and you keep me going on the days when the research is either dark or simply frustrating. Without all of you, the histories we have uncovered simply wouldn't be told.

And lastly, to my family, thank you for your support and your interest. Your enthusiasm and your reactions to the hidden histories I have uncovered make it all worthwhile.

ABOUT THE AUTHOR

An engaging and thought-provoking public speaker, Brian Sheffey has expertise in mid-Atlantic and Southern American genealogical research, with an emphasis on the intersection of white, black, and Native American genealogy. He has used his knowledge to solve cases of unknown parentage from Colonial America to the present day, utilizing DNA and paper-trail evidence.

Brian has deep family roots in colonial Virginia and the Carolinas, the Powhatan, Choctaw, and Creek tribes, and the colonial Quaker guarantees in the mid-Atlantic region. His passion for genealogy was inspired by his father and his father's drive and desire to discover the story of his family. This understanding inspires his work to help others uncover their own ancestral stories. He combines over 20 years of experience in marketing research, entertainment industry experience, and academia with a passion for genealogical research and a unique ability to solve seemingly impossible cases. His primary research interests include cases of unknown parentage, such as identifying the white progenitors of mulatto family lines; and triangulating answers to difficult genealogical questions using traditional records and genetic evidence.

Behind his passion for research lies the belief that genealogy is an opportunity to link with Americans from different backgrounds to enable them to connect with each other and make contacts around the globe.